Document Strategy Design Workbook

Document Strategy Design Workbook

Kevin Craine

MC² Books
Grapevine, Texas

Many of the identifiers used by vendors of software, hardware, manufactured items, services, and other products are trademarked, service marked or registered trademarks of the companies that sell them. We recognize the claims of all of the manufacturers identified in this work.

ISBN: 1-893347-07-9

Copyright ©2002 by Kevin Craine

All rights reserved. No part of this publication may be reproduced, stored in a retrieval system, or transmitted, in any form or by any means, electronic or mechanical, including photocopying, recording, or acquisition by any other form of information recording or storage device, without prior written permission by the Publisher.

MC² Books is a member of the McGrew + McDaniel Group

Jacket Design by Tamara Grigsby

First Printing, July 2002

The author and publisher have made every effort to ensure the accuracy of the information and examples shown in this book. However, this book is sold without any warranty, expressed or implied. Neither the author nor the publisher will be liable for any damages caused or alleged to be caused by the inforamtion in this book. The opinions expressed in this book are those of the authors and not necessarily those of the publisher, booksellers or distributors.

MC² Books are available at special discounts for bulk purchases.

Please contact McGrew + McDaniel Group:

3207 S. Geneva St.
Denver, CO 80231

Fax: +1 720 282 3129

Email: info@mcgrewmcdaniel.com

URL: www.mc2books.com

To Allyson

Contents

Contents vii

Preface ix

Acknowledgements xi

Introduction 1

Baseline Assessment 5

Documents, Technology & People 17

Problems and Solutions 29

Constructing a Project Proposal 51

Managing Change, Navigating Corporate Culture 59

Project Planning and Implementation 65

Conclusion 75

Preface

Since its release in October of 2000, thousands of copies of *Designing a Document Strategy* have been sold in over 25 countries around the world and the book has gained universal acceptance throughout the document processing industry. Hundreds of document industry professionals have successfully executed the methods in the book to design working strategies and improve their document technology processes. A number of well-known vendor organizations have endorsed and utilized the book as well, and the text is required reading at several universities in the United States, Canada and in Europe. I am pleased that my work has resonated with so many of my industry colleagues, corporate executives and the academic community. The broad acceptance of the book has been overwhelming.

As a result, a growing demand for a workbook to accompany *Designing a Document Strategy* developed. While the original book contains a complete program, including templates and examples to facilitate the design of a document strategy, many "document strategy designers" wanted a quick reference guide and a place to compile their work. Industry vendors wanted a workbook to supply to customers. University professors wanted a summarization of the process and open-ended forms to facilitate classroom instruction. With these desires defined – and my publisher willing – the *Document Strategy Design Workbook* was born.

This workbook does not attempt to revisit or abridge the entire content in *Designing a Document Strategy*. The intent is to provide summaries of the salient approaches and supply simple worksheets to compile your findings and bring together the information and perspective needed to "sell" your strategy and construct a meaningful implementation plan.

To make proper use of this workbook you will need to refer to the original text. If you don't already have a copy, it is available at **www.document-strategy.com**.

Acknowledgements

I would like to thank the many readers and supporters of *Designing a Document Strategy*. I am thankful for Pat McGrew and Bill McDaniel at MC² Books and their abiding encouragement and honest partnership. I am indebted also to Paul Telles and Lisa Magnuson for their valuable assistance and friendship. Thanks also to Ron Brent, Marll Thiede, Ken Waddell, and the rest of the team at *Document Processing Technology* magazine for their support of my work. I must acknowledge also my colleagues at Regence BlueCross BlueShield, however the concepts and notions expressed herein represent my own opinion and do not necessarily represent the views of my employers. Finally, I am thankful for my family's love, support and understanding during the creation this book and during the many related ventures associated with my work.

► Introduction ◄

How to use this workbook

The *Document Strategy Design Workbook* is intended as an accompaniment to the book, *Designing a Document Strategy*. To make proper use of this workbook you will need to refer to the original text (available at **www.document-strategy.com**) where the concepts and approaches are explained and explored in more detail. Also, not all of the notions presented in the original text are covered here, so having a copy of the book is important for a full understanding of the assessment and design process prescribed.

The chapters in this workbook follow the five-phase Document Strategy Model presented in detail in *Designing a Document Strategy*. Each chapter starts with some assigned reading from the original text. Read this before moving into practical application through the use of the forms provided in the workbook. By following these assignments you will perform a systematic assessment of the fundamental business needs, performance pressures and process measures within your organization. You will target your most important documents and understand the process and technologies that create them. You will identify and understand the needs of the people who create, use and care about your documents.

Once you have completed the process outlined in this workbook you will be prepared for the critical decision-making and action planning needed to design a document strategy that makes sense for your particular situation and organization. You will gain the perspective and build the justification needed to "sell" your strategy to executive decision-makers and co-workers. You will validate your ideas and develop solutions that will result in real-world, bottom-line benefits for your organization. If you are a student, you will find this workbook a useful tool to prepare yourself for a career in the document industry – an industry with a burgeoning need for more holistic and strategic approaches to document, data and information management.

I encourage you also to join the "Document Strategy Online Forum" where document industry professionals from around the world gather to share their experiences, challenges and successes using a Web-based discussion database.

To join visit **www.document-strategy.com**.

Overview of the Document Strategy Model

Assignment: Read Chapter Two of *Designing a Document Strategy* (pages 15 – 21).

The Document Strategy Model is not intended to be linear. The overlapping circles of the model demonstrate that the steps often will overlap. You might find that you don't need to follow every step in detail, or there are times when you must retrace your steps back to square one. The framework can and should be adapted to suit your particular situation, organization or requirement. The DS Model helps to provide focus, avoid pitfalls and save valuable time and energy.

The Document Strategy Model

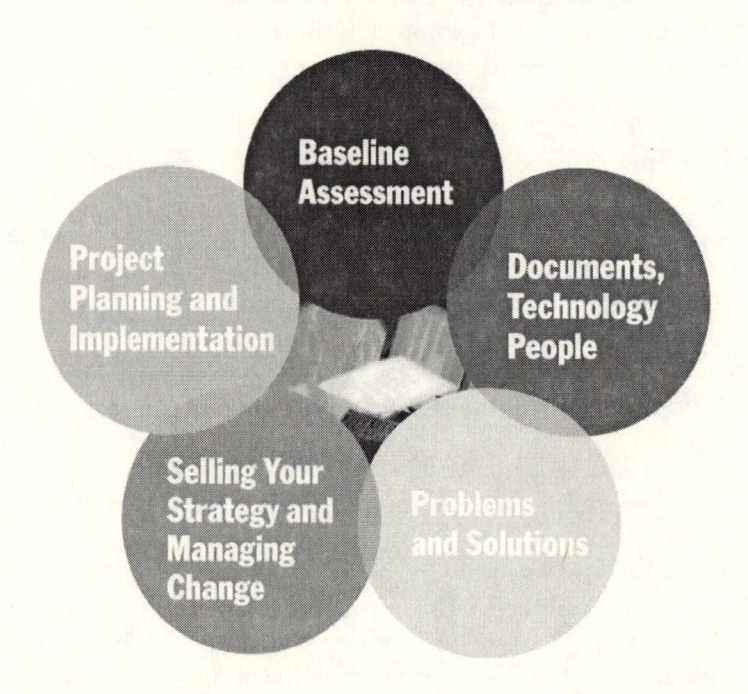

- Baseline Assessment
- Project Planning and Implementation
- Documents, Technology People
- Selling Your Strategy and Managing Change
- Problems and Solutions

Baseline Assessment

The process starts with a Baseline Assessment that asks: Where are you, and where do you need to go? The assessment helps you "get located" by establishing a baseline about the purpose and direction of your organization, the needs, pressures and constraints it must satisfy and manage, and the hard numbers that measure its success. A Baseline Assessment also explores the most pressing problems that challenge your company and the most advantageous opportunities for improvement.

Documents, Technology and People

One way to keep your document strategy manageable, yet comprehensive is to view it through three basic frames of reference: documents, technology and people. At the most fundamental level, this is what a document strategy is all about. *Documents* are the subject of your strategy, *technology* is how you produce them, and *people* are why they exist. You will chart a meaningful course for your strategy by compiling a list of target documents, assessing how those documents are produced, and understanding the needs of the people who use and care about them.

Problems and Solutions

In order to be successful, your document strategy must provide solutions to the problems in your current processes. It is impossible to determine appropriate solutions until you understand and define the problems that exist. You will do this by comparing how things are with the way they should be. You will examine how your current processes perform and determine whether or not they perform in ways that meet the needs of your organization. Once you have defined the problems that exist and determined their root cause(s), you will identify and select the best solutions to solve those problems and improve your processes.

Selling your Strategy and Managing Change

Next, the Document Strategy Model explores the critical need to sell your strategy and manage change. Your efforts are not likely to be successful if you do not enlist the support of decision-makers and co-workers. Selling your strategy requires a solid business case as well as the ability to "speak the language" of the people you aim to convince. You will do this by constructing a financial analysis and a formal proposal for your ideas and solutions. You will also examine ways to enlist the support of co-workers and decision-makers.

Change and corporate culture significantly influence your document strategy. To better manage change you will explore the roles people play in a successful change initiative. You will also consider the natural and emotional reactions that people have during times of change. In addition, you will examine the cultural characteristics of your organization and how they will influence your efforts.

Project Planning and Implementation

Project planning and implementation is where all of your assessment, analysis and planning must come together. You must develop a project plan that will be clearly understood by everyone involved and guide your efforts to a successful implementation. You must challenge your assumptions, test your solutions and demonstrate your success.

► 1: Baseline Assessment ◄

Assignment: Read Chapter Three of *Designing a Document Strategy*. (pages 23 – 37).

A sailor must know two things before he can chart a course: his current location and the location of where he wants to go. When mapping a document strategy, you must also understand two things in order to make the right directional decisions: *Where are you now? Where do you want to go?*

Do this by performing a Baseline Assessment. This assessment provides a starting point. It provides a sense of direction and helps to make the process of designing a document strategy more manageable and measurable. Most importantly, a Baseline Assessment makes certain that your plans are closely linked to the fundamental needs and objectives of your particular organization. The more closely your strategy is tied to these basics, the more likely it will be given sponsorship, support and funding, and the more likely your efforts will result in meaningful improvement.

Step One: Measures, Pressures and Constraints

Definitions

Hard Numbers. These are the numbers found in operating budgets, expected growth targets, anticipated rates of return, desired customer retention, containment of administrative costs, and so on. Investigate numbers reported to senior management and divisional vice presidents. Look for figures found in quarterly financial reports and performance projections. Seek out statistics that measure corporate performance.

Competitive Pressures. What are the competitive pressures your company must manage? Understand marketplace competitors and how they challenge the success of your company. Internal competition is also an important, so examine the internal climate of your company as well.

Operational Pressures. These are the pressures of conducting business every day. Analyze labor and workforce issues, difficulties with logistics and locations, poor product quality, material shortages or manufacturing errors.

Constraints, Requirements and Expectations. These are the formal requirements and expectations your company must meet and are often mandatory aspects of doing business set fourth by government and regulatory agencies. Examine the commitments outlined in contracts, settlements and agreements. Include ethical and societal expectations that can critically influence your organization.

Baseline Assessment Worksheet – Step 1.

Understand the key business measures, pressures and constraints that your organization must satisfy and manage. Use additional sheets as needed.

List the "hard numbers" and corporate measures that gauge company performance:

1.

2.

3.

4.

5.

List the business pressures your company must manage:

1.

2.

3.

4.

5.

List the constraints, requirements and expectations that your organization must live with each day:

1.

2.

3.

4.

5.

Other:

By completing these tasks you will conduct a comprehensive yet manageable assessment of your organization's key "needs, pressures and measures." Once you understand *where you are*, you can then determine *where you need to go* and then chart a meaningful course for your document strategy.

Case Example: XYZ Laboratories

Review the case example of XYZ laboratories covered in more detail in *Designing a Document Strategy* (page 30). Their Baseline Assessment uncovered the following data. View this information through the perspective of your document strategy. Are these factors similar to the ones that may be found in your organization? Are there others that should be added to your assessment? What are the factors that describe your particular situation and can point the direction for your document strategy?

Hard Numbers	*Hard Numbers*
Realize a 7% growth in annual sales.	How can a document strategy help to increase sales and mitigate increases in operating expense?
Keep operating costs below a 4% increase.	What contributions might documents make to these percentage targets? How can that be demonstrated?
Competitive Pressures	*Competitive Pressures*
Maintain production quality at less than 1% defect rate.	How can a document strategy assist with quality control and help keep production costs down?
Maintain prices 8% - 10% below market competitors.	How can documents help track defects and eliminate waste?

Operational Pressures	**Operational Pressures**
Maintain operations at a high rate of efficiency (approx. 90%) while reducing workforce by 2%. Minimize inefficiencies in workflow between diverse locations (due to merger and acquisition of several competitors in different locations).	How are people spending their time with documents? How can documents eliminate redundant or unnecessary work? How can documents help connect the various workgroups within the company and bring people together? How can documents prompt efficient actions and guide workflow.
Constraints, Requirements and Expectations	**Constraints, Requirements and Expectations**
Gain regulatory approval of four new products. Comply with government standards on all products. Improve the corporate image in local community.	What role do documents play in the process to gain regulatory approval? How do documents support efforts to comply with standards? How can documents build a positive image of the company in the community?

You can quickly determine a direction for your document strategy by exploring these basic factors that drive your business. How can your document strategy assist with these important success measures? Ideas for improvement will come more quickly with a review of these fundamentals. Solutions will become more apparent once your baseline is established. If you do nothing more than examine these aspects of your organization you will be well on your way to designing a document strategy that will make a difference in the real-world.

Step Two: Objectives and Strategies

Objectives and strategies link corporate performance to the bottom-line. To determine your direction, you must understand how your document strategy can benefit the specific and measurable objectives of your firm.

Definitions

Long-Term Objectives and Grand Strategy. Long-term objectives are the results needed over a multi-year period. Focus on areas like profitability, return on investment, competitive position, market leadership, productivity, and customer satisfaction and retention. A grand strategy is how your firm intends to meet its long-term objectives. Focus on how your objectives are to be achieved, when they should be achieved, and to what degree they should benefit the company.

Short-Term Objectives and Operating Strategies. Short-term objectives are the results needed within one year. While somewhat similar in nature to long-term objectives, the outcomes associated with short-term objectives will be more specific and more immediately measured. Most of the operational and functional strategies in your organization will be set to achieve short-term objectives. The culmination of those achievements should be a part of the framework of your document strategy.

Baseline Assessment Worksheet – Step 2.

Examine the specific *objectives and strategies* that are defined in your company business plan. Use additional sheets as needed.

List your company's long-term objectives and summarize your overall strategy:

1.

2.

3.

4.

5.

List your organization's short-term objectives and summarize your operational strategies:

1.

2.

3.

4.

5.

List the specific ways your company tracks the achievement of these objectives:

1.

2.

3.

4.

5.

Other?

Case Example: XYZ Laboratories

Consider these short- and long-term goals and objectives that measure the performance of XYZ Laboratories (see page 33 in *Designing a Document Strategy*). Are these measures similar to the ones you may find in your organization? What are the specific ways your firm tracks the achievement of its objectives? What are the measures that should be a part of your assessment?

Customer satisfaction

An index for satisfaction of surveyed customers based on a 10-point scale with 10 being "extremely satisfied."

    2002 baseline: 8.1

    2003 objective: 9.3

    2004 objective: 9.7

Customer retention

Describes the number of lost customers versus new customers based on "zero defect" – one hundred percent new customers, zero percent lost customers.

    2002 baseline: 82/18

    2003 objective: 91/9

    2004 objective: 97/3

Sales conversion on new customers

Describes the number of newly attained customers versus the number of prospective customers.

    2002 baseline: 21%

    2003 objective: 30%

    2004 objective: 35%

Revenue growth

A percent indicator of increased or decreased revenue over the prior year.

    2001 - 2002 baseline 7.8%

    2002 - 2003 objective 10%

    2003 - 2004 objective 15%

Operating expense

The percentage of operating expense versus gross revenue.

    2002 baseline: 12%

    2003 objective: 10.5%

    2004 objective: 8.5%

On-time performance – product to market

    2002 baseline: 83%

    2003 objective: 94%

    2004 objective: 100%

Regulatory Licensing

Achievement of license and accreditation by regulatory body.

    2002 baseline: 1-year

    2003 objective: 5-year

    2004 objective: renew 5-year

> View these objectives with your document strategy in mind. Do your objectives resemble those at XYZ? What objectives should be added to your list? How do your objectives influence the design of your document strategy? The key is to discover how your document strategy can bring about a positive result for your organization in the most fundamental terms. How can it serve your specific goals and objectives? How can a strategy assist with your short-term objectives? How can it help to fulfill your organization's overall strategy? If you can answer these questions in quantifiable and specific terms, you are well on your way. Follow these compass points as you map your document strategy.

Step Three: Mission and Vision

Definitions

The mission and vision of your organization are the foundation upon which it develops specific objectives and strategies. For your document strategy to be of lasting benefit it must tap into the most important aspects of your company's mission and serve the vision of executive policy-makers.

Mission. A mission statement is a proclamation about your organization's driving purpose, philosophy and goals. It might also define your products and services, and describe specific methods or technologies your firm will use to provide those products and services. It might also express the types of markets that are most important, who your core customers are, and the internal competencies needed to do business.

Vision. Corporate vision is a general strategy for achieving its mission. Many organizations develop vision statements that describe where the organization is headed and what it intends to be. A vision statement depicts a future that would not happen by itself. Corporate vision articulates the basic characteristics that shape your organization's approach to doing business.

Baseline Assessment Worksheet – Step 3.

Understand the *mission and vision* **of your organization. Use additional sheets as needed.**

List are the reasons your company exists…what it does and why:

1.

2.

3.

4.

5.

List the specific way your company envisions its success:

1.

2.

3.

4.

5.

List the specific initiatives underway to achieve your company's mission and vision:

1.

2.

3.

4.

5.

Other?

The value of understanding your organization's mission and vision is that you will develop a relatively comprehensive view of your organization. How your mission and vision touch you personally is probably through the impact of your hard numbers and business pressures, but be clear about the links between your document strategy and your business. What are the specific initiatives underway to achieve your company's mission and vision? Who is ultimately responsible for seeing those initiatives through? How can a document strategy help fulfill those initiatives?

Good decisions are based on good data, and your objective is to get as complete a picture of your organization as you can. Develop a comprehensive view that includes an understanding of your organization's measures, pressures and constraints, as well as your company's mission and vision. You need this information in order to make informed directional decisions and to be able to write your business case in terms that decision-makers will understand and appreciate.

▶ 2: Documents, Technology & People ◀

Assignment: Read Chapter Four of *Designing a Document Strategy*. (pages 40 – 63).

Continue your assessment in three specific areas of inquiry: documents, technology and people. These three elements are essentially the "what, how and who" of your document strategy: *what* documents are most important, *how* they are produced, and *who* cares about how they perform in the process.

Documents

Determine your target documents

Documents are, naturally, the subject of your strategy. In order to increase the strategic value and tactical effectiveness of your documents, it stands to reason that you should determine which ones are the most important to your organization. Using the information you collected in your Baseline Assessment, identify a "vital few" target documents that offer the highest return and the best likelihood for success in terms of meeting the needs of your organization.

Case Example: XYZ Laboratories

As you follow the XYZ Laboratories case study in *Designing a Document Strategy*, (pages 45 – 47) you will notice that the firm has approximately fifty thousand documents that are used within their enterprise. They framed their investigation using the following functional categories, and then assessed the number of documents that are used within each business function.

Total Enterprise Documents   50,000   100%

Core Functions	Number of Core Documents
Marketing	2,500
Finance	2,000
Research	3,200
Production	800
Human Resources	<u>1,500</u>

Total Core Documents   10,000   20%

XYZ determined that only twenty percent of the total number of documents in their organization actually drives the core functions of their business. Ten thousand of the original fifty thousand are "core documents." Ten thousand is still a daunting number, however, so XYZ takes the next step by asking: Of this twenty percent, which documents are absolutely essential for our business to run? Which have the capacity to bring business to its knees? If ranked in priority, which documents rise to the top?

Core Functions	Mission-Critical Documents
Marketing	475
Finance	300
Research	575
Production	350
Human Resources	<u>300</u>

Mission-Critical Documents   2,000

The surviving two thousand documents are seen as "mission-critical" for XYZ Laboratories. Out of ten thousand core documents, only two thousand remain.

But two thousand documents can still seem very overwhelming. Consequently, XYZ distills the list even further to the essential "vital few" they feel they should target for their strategy. While they agree that there are other documents that also need attention, the team at XYZ finalizes their list this way:

Core Functions	Target Documents
Marketing	New product literature
	Customer letters
Finance	Monthly customer statements
	Large account billings
Research	Patent research reports
	Regulatory compliance documentation
Production	Work request tracking reports
	Inventory and production reports
Human Resources	Employee benefits reports
	Hiring and termination forms

Number of Target Documents **10**

The XYZ example illustrates how you can reduce the seemingly overwhelming scope of your document strategy to a more manageable project by concentrating only on those documents that are vitally important. While there may be literally thousands of documents within your enterprise, you may find that there are a relative few that are absolutely essential.

Assess Your Situation

Perform an assessment similar to the one used in the XYZ case study by answering the following questions:

- Which documents have the biggest influence on your numbers and measures?
- Which help manage the needs, pressures and constraints of doing business?
- Which contribute to meeting your specific goals and objectives?
- Which serve your overall mission and vision?
- Which are the most troublesome in terms of support, errors and efficiency?
- Which are the most costly to create, produce and process?
- Which have the biggest influence on customer satisfaction?
- Which have the biggest influence on efficiency?
- Which serve important strategic initiatives?

The answers help pair down their two thousand mission-critical documents to a short list of the most vital documents – *the most essential with the most potential.*

Perform a similar analysis of your organization using the worksheet provided below. Which documents make up your "vital few" target documents? If you could pick only a handful of documents to target for your document strategy, which ones would they be? Which documents deserve to be on your "top ten" list?

Select your target documents by returning to your **Baseline Assessment**. Which documents have the greatest influence on the success of your organization? Which ones play a part in realizing your firm's objectives and vision? Which are in most need of improvement, are the most troublesome, or provide the most potential return for your effort?

Target Documents Worksheet

Determine the "vital few" documents that are the most important for your organization. Use additional sheets as needed.

List the documents used in your critical business functions:

1.

2.

3.

4.

5.

List the documents that have the highest potential return on your effort or present the most troublesome problems:

1.

2.

3.

4.

5.

List the documents that have the best probability for success:

1.

2.

3.

4.

5.

Other:

Technology

Examine the process

Now that you have selected your target documents, your next step is to examine the technology used to create, produce and process those documents. What are the requirements of the process? How do things get done, and why? What are the strengths and weaknesses of your current technology? Your aim is to get a brief, yet comprehensive view of your current capabilities. Concentrate on your target documents and examine the technology used to produce them.

Document Life Cycle

One way to approach this assessment is to follow your target documents through their life cycle. While the life cycle of a document can be described in various ways, assume your documents have these phases in common:

Creation: Assembling information into a purposeful design.

Production: Presenting and delivering a document on paper or in digital form.

Revision: Reusing or updating a document, or parts of it, for an assortment of reasons.

Archive: Storing a document for later retrieval.

Retirement: A document is deemed obsolete and is destroyed or deleted.

Document Lifecycle Worksheet

Follow each of your target documents through this life cycle. What are the technological aspects and requirements of the process? Use additional sheets as needed. Add or delete questions as needed for your particular situation.

Creation - Where does the information come from that populates the document?

- Which data files contribute to the document?
- What databases are used?
- How is variable and static information used?
- Does the information reside on a mainframe? A server? A disk? Other?
- How is the format designed?
- What layout software is used?
- Are templates or overlays used?
- How are text and graphic elements put together?

Production - How is the document produced, processed and presented?

- Is the document issued on paper? On screen? On disk? On the Web? To a hand-held device? All of the above?
- What software and hardware is used in the process?
- What protocols, programs and languages facilitate production?
- Does the document exist in multiple formats (e.g., paper and digital) or multiple languages?
- Is equipment overworked or under utilized?
- Are there seasonal fluctuations that impact production (e.g., tax season, year end, etc.)?

Revision - How are revisions to the document achieved?

- Are revisions handled the same way as the original creation?
- Are the original authors revising the document, or someone else?
- When revisions are made, what happens to the original version? How are revisions tracked and monitored?
- Does the document get revised and re purposed for other uses?

Archive - How is the document saved and archived?

- In what format is the document archived (e.g., paper or digital)?
- What software and hardware is used to store and access it?
- What protocols, programs and languages are used?
- When retrieved, will the document resume its prior format or be used in different ways?
- Are there legal ramifications for the archived document? Is the document retained in an archive or eliminated?
- Will pieces of the original document live on in other incarnations?

Adapt this process to fit your particular situation. Remove questions that do not apply and add questions of your own and from your co-workers. Remember to concentrate only on your target documents. Bring together a profile that reflects how these documents are created and processed.

Reviewing the technology used to produce your target documents will help you gauge the strengths and weaknesses of your current process and judge the potential improvement benefits of new and developing technology.

People

Know your "Document Constituency"

The people who create, use and care about your documents are the best people to provide the finer points of navigation for your strategy. Who can better describe which documents are important, how they are used, how they perform and how things could be better?

The notion of a "document constituency" is explored in more detail in *Designing a Document Strategy* (pages 56 – 62). The people who make up your document constituency are the people who use your documents, have responsibility for their existence and have a stake in how well they perform. You can identify members of your document constituency by using these four categories:

> *Authors:* the writers, composers and content providers, both intentional and implied.
>
> *Producers:* the creators, producers and processors of your documents.
>
> *Stakeholders:* the people who have a stake in the performance of your documents.
>
> *Readers:* the people who use, read, and react to your documents.

Each of these people has a different set of needs, expectations and constraints and the activities and requirements of the people within your constituency will influence and determine both the message of your documents and the medium used to deliver them. Document attributes are entirely determined by the people in your document constituency.

Document Constituency Worksheet

Who are the authors, producers, readers, and stakeholders of your target documents?

List the authors of your target documents:

1.

2.

3.

4.

5.

List the producers of your target documents:

1.

2.

3.

4.

5.

List the stakeholders of your target documents:

1.

2.

3.

4.

5.

List the readers of your target documents:

1.

2.

3.

4.

5.

The needs, constraints and requirements of your document constituency will guide your decisions and actions within your document strategy. Additionally, by consulting these people during the design of your document strategy, you will be more likely to have their support and participation in whatever changes you propose. Ultimately, by identifying your document constituency and understanding their respective needs and constraints, you will be more likely to construct meaningful and effective tactics within your strategy.

Case Example: XYZ Laboratories

Return to the XYZ Laboratories case example in *Designing a Document Strategy* (page 61). Below is the constituency identified for XYZ's customer statements, a crucial target document. They begin by asking: Who creates this document, who uses it, and who cares about its performance? From there, they segment their document constituents into authors, producers, stakeholders and readers. Note that departments as well as specific people are identified as document constituents. Who are the members of your document constituency?

Authors

Information Services:	Cathy Hiatt – Programmer
Finance:	Debbie Faunce – Accounts Payable
Customer Services:	Lynette Cranford – Administrative Specialist
Marketing:	Anthony Zel – Regional Product Representative

Producers

Information Services:	Kevin Rogers – Corporate Forms Analyst
	Sandra Strait – Print Shop Supervisor
Administration:	Roland Reiniger – Mail Services Supervisor

Stakeholders

Customer Services:	Cindy Johnson – Manager
Information Services:	Tammy Rivas – Manager
Finance:	Brandon Woods – Manager, Accounts Payable
Marketing:	Lisa Magnuson – Regional Manager

Readers

XYZ Internal Personnel: Shawn Rosen – Accounts Receivable

External Customers: Billing Clerks / Accounts Payable

Department Secretaries

Shipping and Receiving Clerks

Purchasing staff

Departmental Managers

In the end, *documents* are created with *technology* to be used by *people,* so it makes sense that these three factors surface as guiding beacons for your document strategy. Mapping the course of your plans from these perspectives will help direct the latitude of your effort and ensure that your design process is comprehensive yet manageable. As a result, your directional decisions will not only be possible but practical, and more likely to lead you to a more profitable destination.

▶ 3: Problems and Solutions ◀

Assignment: Read Chapter Five of *Designing a Document Strategy*. (pages 64 – 98).

At this point you should have a better idea of "where you are and where you need to go." The question now becomes: How exactly will you get there? No matter how clearly you map your destination, the key to arriving is to chart and execute specific ways to proceed. A reminder: Properly identifying problems and their solutions is a large and important part of the document strategy design process prescribed herein. As mentioned previously, this workbook is intended as a supplement to *Designing a Document Strategy* and the elements of this portion of the Document Strategy Model are described in more detail in the original text. To effectively proceed you will need to refer to both the workbook and the original text.

Identify Problems. What problems exist in the performance of your target documents? What are the gaps between the objectives of your organization, the needs of your document constituency and the performance of your document process? How do these problems prevent you from being successful, and why do they exist?

Identify Solutions. How will you navigate from your current location to your desired destination? The solutions you choose embody the strategic direction of your plan, so identify solutions that make the most sense for your situation by following this four-step process:

1. Create a document flow chart.
2. Evaluate the process.
3. Define problems and determine causes.
4. Select solutions and plan specific actions.

Document Flow Chart

One secret to the success of your document strategy is to spend the time to step back and examine the process used to create and produce your target documents. Construct a document flow chart that shows the path a document travels throughout your organization. Diagram the process and examine the performance of each of your target documents. Identify the steps along the way and the major tasks, actions and events associated with each step.

Elements of a flow chart

Symbol	Name	Explanation
⬭	Elongated Circle	Shows the beginning and ending points of a flow chart.
☐	Box	Represents the steps in your document workflow. Include a short description of the task performed, the function served, or the person or department who receives your document.
◇	Diamond	Indicates any decision point. Include a question that can be answered *yes* or *no*. The direction your document will flow depends on the answer.
→	Straight Arrow	Shows direction of document flow.
⇝	Zigzag Arrow	Shows an electronic data transfer.

Chart the flow of your target documents

Select a document from your list of target documents and build a flow chart using the symbols above. Arrange the symbols of your flow chart so that they accurately illustrate the steps in your document's journey. Identify the major tasks that are dependent on your document. Indicate the equipment and technologies used at each point in the flow. Make note of the people or departments that receive, read and use each document. Ask questions such as:

- Where/when does your target document originate?
- To what points does your document travel?
- What are the major tasks that are dependent on your document?
- What equipment and technology is used at each major step?
- Is your document "translated" from one "language" to another?
- Which departments use your document and how is information converted into action?
- Does your document travel outside your organization?
- Which decisions link documents with people?
- What functions require technology and people to interact effectively?

This is by no means a comprehensive list of questions. Add questions that have meaning for your particular situation.

Document Flowchart Worksheet

Select a document from your list of target documents and build a flow chart using the symbols above. (Use additional sheets or larger poster paper as needed.)

Case Example: XYZ Laboratories

Continue to follow the XYZ Laboratories case example in *Designing a Document Strategy* (page 72). This flow chart examines the process associated with their monthly customer billing statements – a key target document. The flow chart shows the flow of the statement from the time that monthly customer data is generated until the statements are printed and routed to the mail room.

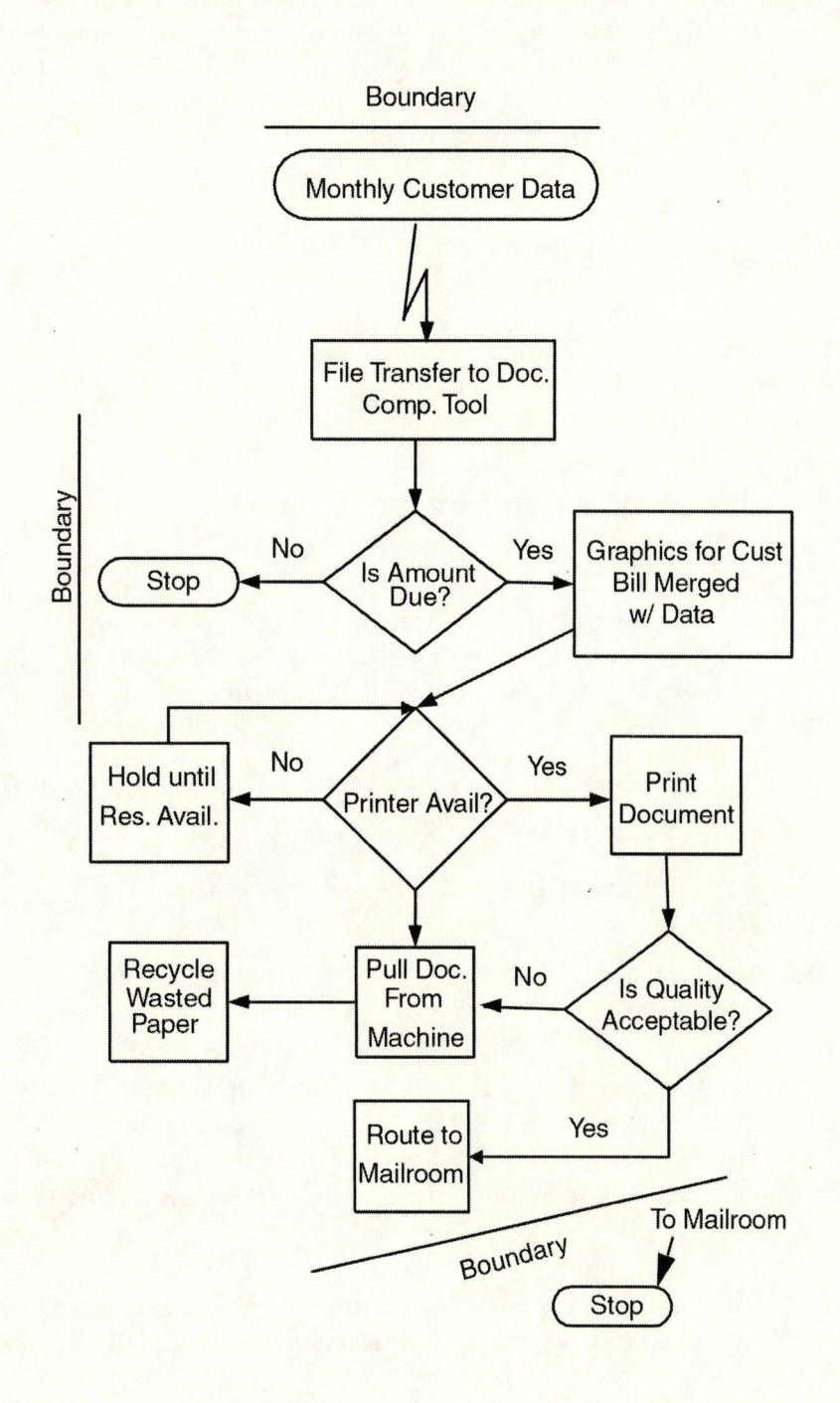

Apply this to your situation

This example is fairly limited in scope and intended only to provide a brief illustration of a document flow chart. As you might imagine, a more complicated document flow that encompasses broader boundaries will take time and effort to put together. You must decide how much detail you will attempt to show in your flow chart as well as how far you will extend the limits of your investigation.

The key is to clearly understand the "as-is" process of your target documents. Creating a flow chart is a remarkably clear way to understand all the elements involved in your process. Unless you understand the overall process you will not be able to determine how to improve it. A flow chart for each target document will lead you to more informed conclusions and beneficial actions for your strategy.

Evaluate the Process

With a flow chart in hand you are now ready to evaluate the process. Do this in three steps: 1, establish a set of expectations; 2, develop process measures; and 3, collect measurement data by observing your "as-is" process in action.

Establish expectations for your target documents

Establishing expectations for each target document is the first step in uncovering the potential problems in your document process. This is where the effort you put into your Baseline Assessment will pay off. How must your documents perform in order to meet your expectations?

One way to assemble your expectations is to return to the concept of "Two Wings" as covered in Chapter One of *Designing a Document Strategy* (page 5). Consider the following categories:

Strategic Wing	Tactical Wing
Customer response	Cost per document
Collecting information	Timeliness and turnaround
Increasing sales	Document quality
Brand awareness	Reducing labor and effort
Perceived quality and confidence	Reduction of errors
Leverage existing information	Maximize investments in infrastructure
Customer satisfaction and loyalty	Reduced operating expense

Are these expectations similar to the ones you might find in your organization? Are there others that should be added to your list? What areas surface as a result of your Baseline Assessment?

Document Expectations Worksheet

Group the expectations for each of your target documents using "strategic" and "tactical" categories. Use additional sheets as needed.

Target Document: _____

Strategic   **Tactical**

1.   1.

2.   2.

3.   3.

4.   4.

5.   5.

6.   6.

7.   7.

8.   8.

9.   9.

10.   10.

Others: Others:

Develop process measures

Process measures provide a way to observe the performance of your document process, uncover the problems that exist and monitor the results of your improvement efforts. Using your flow chart as a guide, place measures at key points in your process. Weigh these measures against the expectations you have set for your target documents to determine whether your process does – or does not – perform as you desire. For more detailed information about process measures refer to pages 78 – 79 in *Designing a Document Strategy*.

Case Example: XYZ Laboratories

The XYZ Laboratories case example (page 80) continues the process with the evaluation of their monthly customer billing statements. Expectations are grouped into the following strategic and tactical categories.

Target document: Monthly Billing Statement

Expectations

Strategic	Tactical
Customer Response	**Cost per document**
Payment received from customer within 10 days or less.	Not to exceed $0.03 (printing cost only)
Accuracy	**Timeliness**
Payment is correct no less than 99% the time.	Document is delivered to mail room of within 24 hours upon receipt of the print job.
Leveraging existing information	**Document quality and errors**
Custom messages and promotional information issued with each bill.	Documents rerun or issued in error not to exceed .01 % of total documents.

To gather meaningful and descriptive data, XYZ put input, in-process and result measures into place.

Process Measures

Process Measures — Results Needed

Input Measures

The percentage of statements with incorrect billing data	No more than 1%

In-Process Measures

The average cost per document.	No more than $.03
The percentage of statements delivered within 24 hours after issue.	Target 100%
The percentage of statements issued with custom message p/month.	Target 100%

Result Measures

The average number of days before customer payment is received.	Under 10 day ave.
The percentage of statements issued with no errors.	No less than 99%
The percentage of statements that are rerun or sent in error.	No more than .01%

Apply to your situation

Are these measures similar to the ones you may find for your target documents? Are there others that should be added to your list? How can you set your expectations and measures using both "strategic" and "tactical" frames of reference?

Document Process Measures Worksheet

Group process measures for each of your target documents using the "strategic" and "tactical" expectations you set previously. Use additional sheets as needed.

Target Document: _____

Strategic	Tactical
1.	1.
2.	2.
3.	3.
4.	4.
5.	5.
6.	6.
7.	7.
8.	8.
9.	9.
10.	10.
Others:	Others:

Collect Process Measurement Data

Many companies do a poor job of systemically collecting appropriate data and analyzing it properly. You can overcome this problem by using your document flow chart to provide an overall picture of your process, then use strategic and tactical perspectives to set your expectations and develop your process measures. The final step is to collect process measurement data over time.

As explained in more detail in *Designing a Document Strategy* (page 83), collecting measurement data is like collecting "reality bytes" about your process. Reality bytes are facts and measurement data that describe how the process *really* works; not how it should work… or how people think it works.

Case Example: XYZ Laboratories

Once again, use the XYZ case example as a template for your own efforts (page 84). XYZ collected the following measurement data that indicates how well the process that creates their target document performs against their specific expectations.

Process Measurement Data

Process measure: The percentage of statements with incorrect billing data.
Result needed: No more than 1%
Result observed: Average of 5%

Process measure: The average cost per document.
Result needed: No more than $.03.
Result observed: Average of $.035

Process measure: The percentage of statements delivered within 24 hours after issue
Result needed: Target 100%
Result observed: Average 98%

Process measure: The percentage of statements issued with custom message p/month.
Result needed: Target 100%
Result observed: Average 78%

Process measure:	The average number of days before customer payment is received.
Result needed:	Under 10 days.
Result observed:	Average of 7 days.

Process measure:	The percentage of statements issued with no print quality errors.
Result needed:	No less than 99%
Result observed:	Average 99.5%

What does this data say about the process at XYZ? Will you find similar results when you investigate the process of your target documents? How does this case example relate to your specific process and situation?

Define Problems and Determine Causes

Consider the axiom: *A problem well defined is a problem half solved.* How does the process that produces your target documents measure up to the expectations you have set for each document? To answer this question you must clearly define your problem, then use a Cause-Effect Diagram to determine why those problems plague your process.

To clearly define your problem ask:

- **Is the problem stated objectively?**

  Your problem statement must not be phrased in such a way that it slants the situation in favor of one solution or another.

- **Is the problem limited in scope?**

  Your statement must define your problem so that it is small enough for you to realistically tackle and solve.

- **Does everyone involved have a common understanding of the problem?**

  Your problem statement must be written so that everyone can understand it.

Refer to *Designing a Document Strategy* (pages 85 - 88) for more detailed discussion about problem statements.

Construct a Cause-Effect Diagram

Once you have clearly defined your problem use a Cause-Effect Diagram (a.k.a., "fish diagram") to determine why it exists. Your aim is to isolate the root cause of the problems you discover and avoid making assumptions that may lead you in the wrong direction.

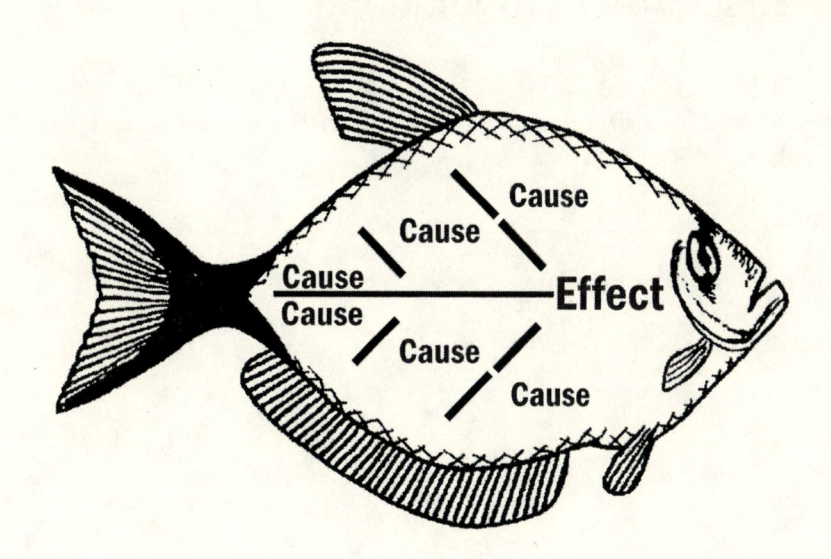

Cause-Effect or Fishbone Diagram

In this sample Cause-Effect Diagram the box at the right end of the diagram (the fish's head) lists the effect of your problem. This effect is the gap between the performance of your document process and the needs of your organization. Categories of potential causes lead off the backbone of the fish. Construct your Cause-Effect Diagram by following these three steps:

1. Identify all potential causes of the problem.
2. Determine the most likely causes.
3. Identify the root cause(s).

Problem Cause-Effect Worksheet

Construct your Cause-Effect Diagram by following these three steps. Use additional sheets as needed.

Target Document: _____

List all potential causes of the problem:

1.

2.

3.

4.

5.

List the most likely causes:

1.

2.

3.

4.

5.

Identify the root cause(s):

1.

2.

3.

4.

5.

Other:

Designing a Document Strategy (pages 93 - 94) discusses how to use brainstorming to identify the potential causes of your problem more easily. The key is to collect as many ideas and perspectives as you can, and add them to your list. Once you have identified the most likely causes, discuss and consider each of them in detail. Eliminate the causes that don't make sense and then consolidate what is left into a short list of likely causes.

Case Example: Customer Order Processing

Consider the problem with customer order processing described in *Designing a Document Strategy* on (pages 85 – 91). The problem was defined in this statement: *"The average time it takes to process customer orders has increased from four days to seven days in the last 12 months. Our desired state is to fulfill orders within three days six months from now and not increase thereafter."* Below is an example of a Cause-Effect Diagram with a few potential causes.

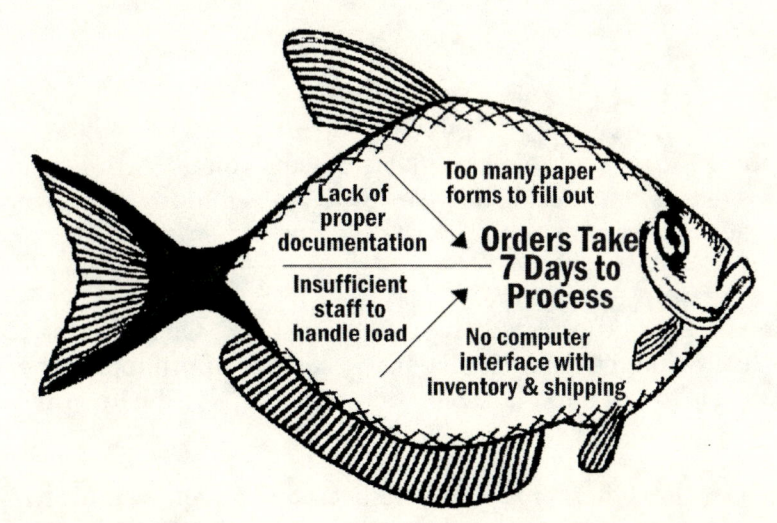

This example only lists four potential causes, but it is not unusual to have many more likely causes for your problem. Make your "fish" as big and long as it needs to be in order to contain all of the likely causes you identify. Trim your list by repeatedly asking: *Why?* For instance, suppose one potential cause for the increase in processing time is a lack of proper documentation.

Ask: *Why is documentation important in the process?*

The answer: *Without the proper documentation the staff will take longer to do their job.*

Ask: *Why does documentation affect the time it takes to do the job?*

The answer: *Because staff members must stop and ask for help..*

Ask: *Why would better documentation reduce the need for assistance?*

The answer: *Because staff members could look up the procedures for themselves.*

Ask: *Why would referring to documentation speed the process?*

In this way you can zero in on the actual origin of your problem. If you do not ask these questions now, you might spend your valuable time and energy working on a solution that does not address the real root cause of your problem. You will find it is not difficult to ask and answer the "Why?" question five or six times before the real root cause of your problem becomes apparent.

Questions to consider while constructing your Cause-Effect Diagram:

- Have you explored all the potential causes?
- Did you get input from the people closest to your problem?
- Are the most likely causes supported by your data?
- Did you ask "Why?" until you got to the real source of your problem?
- Does your problem statement still hold as the best statement to describe your problem?

Select Solutions

The key to finding the best solutions for the problems you uncover is to ask the right questions. This means considering as many potential solutions to your problem as you can possibly generate and then thoughtfully narrow down the possibilities to best one or two alternatives.

Which solutions should be included on your "short list?" Out of all the ideas you have to consider, it is likely that they are not all equally capable of producing the results you want or equally plausible to put into place. The following steps will help you reduce your list to a few of the best options:

1. Develop criteria for your selections and assign weights to each.
2. Apply the criteria.
3. Choose the best four to six solutions.

To determine the criteria to use for selecting the solutions for your short list, make sure that you define each deciding factor clearly. Your criteria must also be rated in terms of importance. Assign a weighting percentage to each criterion so that they total 100 percent. For example:

Ease of implementation	How easy will it be to implement this solution?	20%
Likelihood of success	How likely is it that the solution itself can be successfully implemented?	10%
Effectiveness of Solution	How effective will the solution be in addressing the causes of the problem?	50%
Cost	How much will the solution cost compared to available funding?	20%
Total weighting		**100%**

Rate each possible solution against your criteria. Do this by giving each one a score on a scale of 1 to 10. After you have assigned a score to each factor, multiply the score by the weighting, and add up the scores for each solution. Weighting the criteria helps you choose the best solutions to use for your final decision process.

Solution Criteria Worksheet

Develop criteria for your potential solutions and assign weights to each:

Target Document: _____

Criteria   Defined as: Weight

1.

2.

3.

4.

5.

Other:

Total Weighting:

Weighting the criteria helps you choose the best solutions to use for your final decision process. This is a very effective tool because it compares all your potential solutions objectively and guarantees equal consideration for alternative solutions. Questions to consider when developing your decision criteria:

- Which criteria do you need to consider?
- Are these criteria equally important?
- Does everyone involved have the same understanding of what each one means?
- Do the total weighted scores for each solution seem logical when you compare them with each other?
- Did you choose the solutions with the highest score? If not, why?
- Will you be able to persuade others that this is the right choice? If not, it's probably not the right choice.

Select a final solution

Now that you have a list of potential solutions, you must trim down your choices. Do this by using a Paired-Choice Matrix to choose the best solution from a number of alternatives. This tool ensures that gets objective and equal consideration.

List your solutions on the top, as well as the left side of your matrix. In this example, taken from *Designing a Document Strategy* (page 96), six solutions have been selected (represented as A through F). Begin with the first row (Solution A) and proceed horizontally across the chart, comparing solution A to every solution along the top, one pair at a time. "X's" mark where no choice can be made (e.g., between solution A and solution A). Indicate your preferred solution by placing the corresponding letter in the corresponding column. Repeat this process until each possible pair is evaluated.

	A	B	C	D	E	F	Total
A	x	B	C	D	A	F	1
B	x	x	B	D	B	B	3
C	x	x	x	C	C	F	2
D	x	x	x	x	D	F	1
E	x	x	x	x	x	E	1
F	x	x	x	x	x	x	0
Total	-	1	1	2	0	3	x

Sample Paired-Choice Matrix

To construct your matrix, start with solution A and follow the top of the matrix. Choose between A and B. (In this case solution B was selected.) Continue across the row, making a choice between A and C, A and D, and so on. Repeat the process for each row until you have compared each possible pair – compare B and A, B and C, B and D, and so on. For each row, tally the number of times that solution prevailed. Record those numbers on the right side of your matrix. Tally the scores for each column as well, and record those numbers at the bottom of the matrix. Add the numbers in the right of your matrix with the numbers at the bottom. Whichever solution has the greatest number should be your "best" solution. Use the sample matrix above as a guide.

In the sample matrix above, the results are as follows:

Solution A   -   1 + 0 = 1

Solution B   -   3 + 1 = 4

Solution C   -   2 + 1 = 3

Solution D   -   1 + 2 = 3

Solution E   -   1 + 0 = 1

Solution F   -   0 + 3 = 3

With a total of four, solution B prevails. Solutions C, D and F are viable alternatives.

What happens if you have a tie? If there are three or more options with the same score repeat the process with a smaller matrix that includes only the options that have tied. If you have only two options in a tie, look for other factors that you have not previously considered. Step outside of your main focus to see if your potential solutions provide additional benefits elsewhere. Ask questions such as:

- Did you hold back from evaluating all proposed solutions?
- Did you make a point of thinking outside of your own expertise and experience?
- Did you involve others in the process – especially those who have an interest in getting the problem solved?
- Did you narrow the list to the best four to six possible solutions?
- Do you fully understand each of them?
- Do any of them need to be combined?
- What is the likelihood that your solution will be successful?

The problems you identify and the solutions you select define the course of your document strategy. Use the tools presented in chapter five of *Designing a Document Strategy*, along with this workbook, to strengthen your understanding of the processes that produce your target documents, and then determine the problems (or opportunities) that exist. You will then be in position to select the right solutions for your particular situation.

Paired-Choice Matrix Worksheet

List your solutions below the letters corresponding letters (A,B,C, etc). Follow the instructions above to construct your matrix:

	A	B	C	D	E	F	Total
Solution A							
Solution B							
Solution C							
Solution D							
Solution E							
Solution F							
Total							

► 4: Constructing a Project Proposal ◄

Assignment: Read Chapter Six of *Designing a Document Strategy*.
(pages 99 – 115).

You have gone through the analysis, assessment and evaluation needed to map your plan, now you face perhaps the most difficult task of all: Selling your strategy. Selling your strategy will require a sound business case coupled with the ability to persuasively speak in a language that will resonate with prospective supporters of your plan.

Demonstrate Payback

Designing a Document Strategy discusses various ways to "sell" your strategy (pages 99 – 116). Often this requires that you "speak the language of hard dollars and common sense." To do this you must provide clear justification for the expenditures associated with your plan. The concepts of Net Present Value (NPV) and Internal Rate of Return (IRR) are presented, however, calculating the "payback" of your project is perhaps the most common and easily understood method for calculating return on investment and, consequently, it provides a standard criterion for determining whether to fund a project. Basically, it is the amount of time needed to recover the cost of your project. Your organization may require a specific payback time – typically between one and three years.

Case Example: XYZ Laboratories

Again, return to the case example of XYZ laboratories in *Designing a Document Strategy* (pages 101 - 102). XYZ wants to upgrade equipment in their document production center, but they must justify its purchase in order to get funding approved. A return on investment analysis is needed. Their research has established the following data:

- The current printer prints at 100 pages per minute (.00016 hours per page).
- The print speed of the new printer is 250 per minute. (.00006 hours per page)
- Current print volume is 18 million pages per year.
- The printer operator makes $10.65 per hour including benefits.

XYZ uses this data as a basis to calculate the potential annual savings and prepare a payback analysis to justify the purchase of a new printer.

Their first step is to convert printer speed from pages-per-minute to *hours-per-page*. Pages-per-minute is a common measure of printer speed, but it is necessary to reverse the data and use hours-per-page to calculate payback. This is calculated as follows:

Current printer

100 pages ÷ minute x 60 minutes = 6,000 pages/hour

1 hour ÷ 6,000 pages = .00016 hours per page

Proposed printer

250 pages/minute x 60 minutes = 15,000 pages/hour

1 hour ÷ 15,000 pages = .00006 hours per page

The result of these calculations is actually a *fraction* of an hour per page. (.00016 hours for the old printer, .00006 hours for the new printer.) XYZ now uses the following equation to calculate the cost of using their old printer (current annual cost) as well as the cost of using the new printer (proposed annual cost):

Hours Per Page x Total Pages Per Year x Labor Per Hour   =   Cost

Current Printer Annual Cost

.00016 hours p/page x 18,000,000 pages/year x 10.65/hour   = $30,672

Proposed Printer Annual Cost

.00006 hours p/page x 18,000,000 pages/year x 10.65/hour   = $11,502

To calculate the annual savings that will be realized by using the new printer, XYZ subtracts the proposed annual cost from the current annual cost as follows:

Current Cost	$30,672
Proposed Cost	- 11,502
Annual Savings	$19,170

The amount saved each year is $19,170. By trading in their existing printer, XYZ is able to negotiate a purchase price for the new printer of $50,000.

To determine the time it will take to pay back their investment they divide the cost of the printer by the annual savings.

$$\$50,000 / 19,170 = 2.6$$

The time it will take to pay back the $50,000 investment is **2.6 years**.

This example above is fairly simple, and savvy managers will be quick to point out that additional expense such as hardware maintenance and supplies are not included in the analysis. Regardless, the method for calculating payback is relatively straightforward: Divide your investment expense by your annual savings.

Return on Investment Worksheet

Total your current costs and the proposed costs of your project. Determine your proposed savings (or added expense). Then, divide your investment expense by your proposed savings (or added expense).

Current Costs	Proposed Costs
1.	1.
2.	2.
3.	3.
4.	4.
5.	5.
Total Current Costs:	Total Proposed Costs:
Investment Expense:	Proposed Savings: (or added expense)

Divide your investment expense by your proposed savings (or added expense).

Return on Investment =

Compose a written proposal

Any proposal worth considering must be in written form. Written proposals that are well organized and competently researched are more likely to get attention and acceptance.

The following is an outline for an effective written proposal:

- Executive Summary
- Recommendation
- Discussion
    - Scope
    - Objectives
    - Costs and Benefits
    - Financial Analysis
    - Alternatives
- Suggested Implementation Schedule

Definitions:

Executive summary – Provides a brief background that summarizes the current situation and indicates the reason for your proposition.

Recommendation – What you are asking for and why. Get to your point quickly and be specific. Your proposal must be succinct, have substance and be compelling. Never put your recommendation at the end of your proposal.

Discussion – The body of your proposal that containing the various details of your project.

Scope – Exactly what of your project does and does not cover.

Costs and benefits – A summary of the "hard numbers" and "common sense" that describe why your project should be approved.

Financial analysis – Formal financial analysis vehicles like Return on Investment, Net Present Value or Internal Rate of Return. For more detailed information refer to *Designing a Document Strategy* (pages 101-105).

Alternatives – Other options in lieu of your primary recommendation.

Suggested implementation schedule – Specific milestones and measurements that show how your plan and that it can be accomplished successfully.

Sample Proposal using Payback

Using the previous payback analysis for a new printer, XYZ presents the following written proposal as a request for funding:

April 15, 2003

> To: David Carlson, Vice President of Operations, XYZ Laboratories
> From: Lisa Ness, Manager, Document Services
> Subject: New production printer for the document center

Executive Summary

We use a seven year-old production printer to print bills, statements, checks and an assortment of other critical documents. This machine prints at approximately 100 pages per minute. New printers can print at 250 pages per minute (and more). I propose that we replace our old printer with a new model. This proposal contains the results of my analysis.

Recommendation

I recommend that we spend $50,000 to purchase a new, higher speed, printer. The attached financial analysis shows that we can save an estimated $19,170 per year. The investment has a payback under 3 years (2.6). In addition, there are a number of other benefits that will be realized with the new printer.

Discussion

This new printer will enhance our ability to meet ever-tightening print turnaround expectations. I have visited other companies that have this printer and found that it performs well in similar environments. It will afford us a 150% increase in printing speed.

The impact of installing this new printer will be minimal since it is compatible with existing systems. This is intended as a one-for-one replacement for our current printer (volume 18 million per year). My aim is to shorten our turnaround time by a minimum of 50% and ultimately as much as 150%. There will be no internal support needs since the vendor will remove our old machine and install the new one (included in purchase). Our operators will not need any additional training; the new printer is essentially the same as the old one, only faster.

Please see the attached installation plan. We can install and test the new printer in one week. Disruption to our work will be minimal. The only impact we anticipate is with our weekly statement run (on Mondays), but we feel that we can cover the workload using our other printers and perhaps a few hours of overtime.

As an alternative, we could continue to use our old printer. It requires quite a bit of maintenance, however. Downtime has increased nearly 25% over the past 12 months. On several occasions recently, it has been down for extended periods of time. This is especially troublesome during the first of the month, which is our busiest time. Existing owners of the new printer indicate a dramatic reduction in maintenance and downtime and are more than satisfied with its performance.

We should realize the following benefits:

- We will decrease our turnaround time and increase our print capacity.
- Maintenance and downtime will be reduced.
- The new printer is more technologically up-to-date and will work well with new data processing systems.
- Errors will be reduced due to additional automation features.
- Employee morale will be improved.

Respectfully submitted,
Lisa Ness
Manager, Document Services

Written proposals that are well organized and competently researched are more likely to get attention and acceptance. By presenting your case in writing, you will build management's confidence in your proposal and inspire trust in your abilities.

▶ 5: Managing Change, Navigating Corporate Culture ◀

Assignment: Read Chapter Six of *Designing a Document Strategy*. (pages 116 – 137).

The Roles in a Successful Change Initiative

Once you have the approval to move forward with your strategy, there are five roles that people perform that are critical to your success. For a more in-depth discussion, refer to pages 116 – 122 in *Designing a Document Strategy*.

Definitions - Characteristics of the roles of change:

Change Agent

- Responsible for the implementation of the change.
- Responsible to "educate" the sponsor in terms of what is needed to successfully implement.
- Acts as team leader, keeper of the research and is the expert regarding the change initiative.
- Assembles the needed resources (people, funding and equipment) in order to fulfill change objectives.

Change Sponsor

- Has authority and ability to sanction the change.
- Can commit the needed resources to the project.
- Will apply pressure to overcome barriers and reward supportive performance.
- Will "fly the flag" with other executives and board members as needed.
- Will openly demonstrate support and endorsement of the change.

Change Enabler

- The expert resource needed to implement new technology or changes in the current process.
- Possesses the knowledge and skill to make change happen.
- Acts as a consultant and team member.
- Provides technical and detailed information when needed.
- Provides ideas for improvements and enhancements to existing ideas and solutions.

Change Target

- The individual or group that must actually change.
- Will either embrace or resist change.
- Must assume accountability for the change to be successful.

Sustaining Sponsor

- Responsible for the ongoing process.
- "Takes the ball" once the change has been implemented.
- Responsible for continuous measurement and reevaluation.

Roles of Change Worksheet

List the people who must function in various roles in order for your change to be successful. Remember that you - and others - may need to function in more than one role, "wearing different hats" at different times. Use a separate sheet if needed.

Change Agents - Responsible for the implementation of the change.

Change Sponsors - Has authority and ability to sanction the change.

Change Enablers - The experts needed to implement the change.

Change Targets - The individuals or groups that must assume accountability and embrace the change.

Sustaining Sponsors – The people who will be responsible for the ongoing process.

Others?

Corporate Culture

The culture of your organization can either support your document strategy or work against it as a significant barrier. All organizations have a subjective or invisible culture that will influence your success or failure. Refer to pages 132 – 137 in *Designing a Document Strategy*.

Like the personality of a person, the culture of an organization is not something that is readily apparent at first glance. But after you get to know it, you begin to see the shared beliefs and unwritten ground rules that determine the ways in which your organization will either embrace or resist your document strategy.

Corporate Culture Assessment Worksheet

What Kind of Culture do you have? One of the biggest challenges in trying to understand your own culture is that it is difficult for an insider to see. Observe your organization as if you were an outsider. Use additional sheets as needed.

What gets attention in conversations and in meetings?

Notice people's behavior. Will behaviors contribute to or detract from your efforts?

Examine policies and procedures. Does your culture rely on a few casual guidelines or reams of detailed documentation?

What are the "hero stories?" Who do people talk about with pride and respect? Hero stories model the behavior of employees that is expected by your corporate culture.

Get feedback. Ask employees (especially new employees) to describe the culture and personality of your company or department.

Characteristics of a High Performance Culture

Every company has both positive and negative characteristics. Even companies of similar size in the same industry will have different cultures. There is no perfect culture, but the following chart summarizes some of the characteristics found in high performing organizations. Organizations that embrace, adopt and implement change easily generally exhibit these high performance characteristics, while those that perform less admirably experience the corresponding cultural barriers to change.

Corporate Culture Checklist

Which characteristics does your organization exhibit?

High Performance Characteristics	Cultural Barriers
Empowered people and cross-functional communication.	Turf-building and hierarchical organizational structures.
Open, honest and flowing communication.	Hidden agendas, dishonesty, lack of openness.
Trust and confidence.	Distrust and fear.
Long-term, quality, service and excellence.	Short-term, strictly bottom-line.
Customer-oriented, externally focused.	Task-oriented, internally focused.
"Can-do" spirit.	"Cannot be done" attitude.
Personal responsibility.	Blame and making excuses.
Embracing new ideas.	Prejudiced and judgmental.
Innovation, ingenuity, breakthroughs.	Holding on to the past, resistance to change.
Flexible, fluid and rapidly responsive.	Strict rules and rigid policies.
Win/Win attitude.	Win/Lose attitude.
Others?	Others?

▶ 6: Project Planning and Implementation ◀

Assignment: Read Chapter Seven of *Designing a Document Strategy*. (pages 138 – 157).

Project Planning

A project plan is essential to organize the actions of your document strategy so that they will be clearly understood by everyone involved. A good project plan outlines who will do what and when, and allows you to monitor your project and keep everyone on track. Without a project plan, you cannot measure your progress and results against your objectives. It holds your sponsor accountable for providing the support you need and ensures that change enablers perform as they have promised. You will need to refer to chapter seven of *Designing a Document Strategy* for a more detailed explanation of the concepts presented here.

Project Planning Worksheet

Use the following as framework to organize your project plan.

Project Statement – Describe your project's purpose.

Project Objectives – Describe what will exist when your project is completed.

Assumptions and Facts – Create a list of your assumptions and facts (use separate sheet if needed).

Assumptions   Facts

1.   1.

2.   2.

3.   3.

4.   4.

5.   5.

Your earlier work will serve you well when putting together your project plan. You have already collected the information you need, defined the specific problems to overcome and determined the desired state for improvement. You have selected solutions and established financial data to justify your actions. Now you must challenge your assumptions, verify your facts and outline the action items that need to be completed.

Challenge Assumptions and Verify Facts

Before you layout the specific tasks and timing of your project, it is imperative that you challenge your assumptions and verify your facts. Mistakes or omissions may have been made during your information gathering efforts and conditions may have changed since you first conducted your assessments. By challenging your assumptions and verifying facts, you will confirm the information you are using as a basis for your project is accurate and that everyone is working from the "same page." Do this by creating a list of your assumptions and facts. Use the following example, found in *Designing a Document Strategy* (pages 143 - 145), to guide your efforts in a similar way.

Sample Assumptions / Facts

Assumptions

90% of workstations will not require hardware upgrades to run the new software.

Software support will be provided internally; expertise will be built into current staff.

Document templates will be created to standardize the look of corporate documents.

Production printers will not need to be upgraded for the new software to work.

Facts

Site license will be obtained to lower the total cost of the software.

Upgrades will be handled by the document services staff.

Documents one year old or newer will be translated. All others will be converted as needed.

Updated fonts will be installed at the time the software is installed.

To challenge your assumptions and verify facts, ask questions like:

- Are your assumptions correct?
- Have conditions changed in a way that will affect your assumptions?
- Will your assumptions affect other aspects that you have not considered?
- What happens if your assumptions prove to be inaccurate? Do you have a contingency plan?
- Have you verified that your facts are correct?
- Do you have firm commitments in writing?

Construct an Action Plan

An action plan is a list of all the tasks that need to be performed in order to complete your project. Each task must be relevant to your project goals, be specific yet adaptable, and sequenced in time. To construct your action plan, assign tasks to individuals and teams, then outline the timing of when each task must be completed.

When constructing your action plan, ask questions like:

- What major tasks must be accomplished to complete your project?
- When must these tasks be completed?
- Who should be responsible to accomplish each task?
- How much time can be spent to finish each task?
- What, specifically, will be required from each assignment?

Definitions and Interrelationships of Project Tasks

Dependent tasks - In some cases, the completion of one task depends on the completion of another. You must determine if individual tasks must be performed in sequential order or can be performed as parallel activities. Tasks also can depend on the person conducting them (e.g., Paul is the only one who can do the installation.). In this case, the tasks cannot be performed in parallel because only one person has the expertise or the time to complete the task.

Parallel tasks - When possible, schedule independent tasks to occur simultaneously. You will reduce your total project duration by performing tasks in parallel. You may also, however, increase your risks and incremental costs. Weigh your options and choose the best approach for your particular situation.

Lead- and Lag-Time - You may need to specify lead- or lag-time between tasks. In a *finish-to-start* relationship, an overlap between tasks is called lead-time. This is because the start of the task precedes (or leads) the finish of its predecessor. In a *finish-to-start* relationship, a gap or delay between tasks is called lag-time.

Case Example: XYZ Laboratories Action Plan

Return to the XYZ case study in *Designing a Document Strategy* (page 148) where they construct an action plan to facilitate the installation of new document composition software. The plan includes a project statement along with a list of tasks that must be performed to complete the project. Each task is assigned to an individual or group, and start and end dates have been agreed upon. Dependent tasks are noted at the right when applicable. Note that lag and lead times have been incorporated into the start and end dates, and tasks that can be done in parallel have been indicated at the right.

Action Plan

Project Statement: Implement new document composition software at all production sites by April 15, 2001 at a cost not to exceed $75,000

Project Manager: Lisa Ness **Date:** February 12, 2001

Task	Who	Start	End	Dependent Task
Install software at production sites	Paul	2/11	2/24	None
Test printer connection & file structures	Paul & Doc Svc Staff	2/22	2/23	Software install (parallel tasks)
Create custom files & templates	Allyson	3/1	3/15	Install & testing
Test document Templates	Doc Svc Staff	3/16	3/22	Create custom templates
Pilot document composition & printing	Doc Svc Staff	3/20	4/1	Test templates (parallel tasks)
Verify document quality	Allyson & Doc Svc Staff	3/22	4/10	Pilot document composition (parallel tasks)
Use software for production	Doc Svc Staff	4/10	4/15	Troubleshooting unexpected problems

Construct a similar action plan for your project using the following worksheet. Use additional pages if needed.

Action Plan Worksheet

Project Statement:

Project Manager: _____   **Project Date:** _____

        Task   Who   Start   End   Dependent Task

1.

2.

3.

4.

5.

6.

7.

8.

9.

10.

Outstanding Issues:

Assess your Action Plan

No matter how thoroughly you have constructed your action plan, you cannot anticipate all the outcomes and risks. You can minimize this uncertainty by assessing your action plan before putting it into place. Here are some questions to help assess your plan:

- Are you clear about your long- and short-term project objectives?
- Is your action plan consistent with your earlier assessments?
- Is your plan feasible given known constraints and opportunities?
- Is your action plan realistic given your ability to exercise authority and influence?
- What is the likely impact of your action plan?
- Have you examined the urgency and sequence of the tasks in your plan?
- Have you made sure that early action steps do not unnecessarily or prematurely rule out future alternatives?
- Have you put in place a process to ensure that you will periodically reevaluate and, if appropriate, modify your action plan?

Determine Risks and Develop Contingencies

When planning a project, it is imperative that you consider the likelihood that your project will be successful. What is the probability of success for each step of your action plan? If you can determine the risks associated with your plan and take into account the contingencies ("what if?") you will be better able to plan for them ahead of time. Some questions to consider are:

- Is this a new technology?
- Has this been done before?
- Will conditions change while you are implementing your project?
- What will be the outcome if things go wrong?
- If things go wrong, what will you do?
- What is the probability that your project will be successful? (100%? 50%? 10%?)

Levels of risk and uncertainty vary from project to project. The more complex your project is, the more likely that you will need to "hedge" against the following factors:

Estimates - The best estimates are based on historical data, but predicting the future is far from certain. Complete information is often unavailable. Estimates are not always accurate and may contain errors in financial and technical data.

Design changes - Highly complex tasks and projects may require adjustments along the way. External and internal situations may change over time.

Omissions - Sometimes information is forgotten or overlooked. Information that was not important in the initial stages may be important in later stages.

When making a contingency plan, your goal is to prevent your project from going off course. You will also enrich your entire project planning process by thinking through some alternative routes. Follow these steps to develop a contingency plan:

1. Review your objectives and your action steps. Consider potential problems.
2. Assess the probability that any given problem will occur (e.g., "There is a 50% chance it will occur.").
3. Determine the likely impacts of potential problems (e.g., "What might happen as a result of this?").
4. List your options and alternatives. What are the various ways each risk or problem can be minimized or solved?
5. Develop actions you will take to prevent the potential problem from occurring. If a problem cannot be avoided, develop a contingency or countermeasure.

Evaluate, Document and Demonstrate your Success

Once you have achieved success, demonstrate it. Communicate to your sponsors and co-workers the benefit of your efforts. By doing so, you will be more likely to win continuing support and justification for similar document strategy projects. Some of the steps to follow are:

1. Document the improved process via procedures and operating guidelines.
2. Conduct training on the new process.
3. Gather and provide ongoing feedback to, and from, the people involved.
4. Assure the delivery of promised improvements.

Once your project has been implemented, evaluate the performance of the process or solution to ensure that the improvements you anticipated and promised are actually delivered. This requires careful examination. You may be tempted to skip this step and simply declare success and move on. But assessing and demonstrating your success is essential in order to build your reputation for achievement and encourage sponsors and co-workers to embrace and accept your document strategy efforts in the future. Questions to consider are:

- Did you achieve the outcomes you set for this project? To what extent?
- Did the project end within budget?

- Were costs planned and allocated appropriately?
- Was the return on investment that you anticipated achieved?
- Were areas of opportunities identified and responded to?
- Did the project start and end on time?
- Were problems handled promptly and efficiently?
- Were all of the tasks completed? Were they correctly performed and on time?
- Were the correct resources deployed for this project?
- Did team members have the tools and time they needed to perform their assignments?
- Were resources realistically established in light of the budget or time estimates of the project?

Turn over to Sustaining Sponsors

Even though your project is completed, your job is not over. You must turn over the improved process to a sustaining sponsor. A sustaining sponsor (or sponsors) must assume the responsibility to make certain that the process continues to perform as it should, and recommend and implement changes and adjustments over time. After all, if your project is a success, it is likely that you will be working on further document strategy initiatives and you will not have time to ensure the longevity of your improvements. How well you orchestrate your project's ongoing success is also a sign of effective project management. You must determine what long-term "care and feeding" is needed to foster the continued prosperity of your project and bestow that responsibility on a sustaining sponsor.

▶ 7: Conclusion ◀

Most organizations do not consider themselves to be in the document business. Nevertheless, documents are a second venture for nearly all organizations. By leveraging information contained in documents, communicating effectively and reducing costs, firms that have a document strategy are more likely to have an advantage.

But developing a document strategy is not easy. The aspects to consider are wide-ranging, complicated and elusive. The decision to develop a document strategy can be a paralyzing one and often the quandary becomes, "I know a document strategy is important, but how do I *develop* one?"

Most attempts to answer this poignant problem are either purely technical or primarily conceptual in nature. While jargon and theory can bring to light aspects that one must understand or consider when developing a document strategy, they do not bring the would-be implementer any closer to actually *doing* anything to put the theory into practice. What is needed is a process to follow that will guide decisions and actions that will result in an effective strategy.

This workbook, along with the original text of *Designing a Document Strategy*, provides such a formula – a process that will frame a meaningful strategy tailored for your particular situation. Use the method presented to translate concepts and technology into bottom-line improvements. Fill the gap between theory and practice. Concentrate your efforts in the most important areas to consider.

When it comes to a document strategy, no "one size" fits all. The strategy I need to put into place for my organization is likely to be significantly different than the one needed for your organization. While there may be some basic similarities in how we approach our work or commonalties with the technologies available to improve our processes, in the end our strategic direction can and will vary significantly depending on the specific needs, opportunities, problems, and competitive environment of our respective organizations. While we'd all like a shrink-wrapped solution, designing a meaningful and profitable document strategy requires work, evaluation and action. These are the steps outlined herein.

My intent is not to provide all the answers in a cookie-cutter strategy, but rather to prompt your assessment, decisions and actions in thoughtful ways toward specific improvement goals. I do not suggest that this is the best or only way to craft a document strategy, but the principles have proven effective in several disciplines including Total Quality Management, Organizational Development, Data Processing and Communications.

Since a document strategy will vary for each organization. Some customizing of this work is a must, and I encourage you to transform this approach into actions that are appropriate for your particular situation.

Best of luck and success.

Kevin Craine

kevin@document-strategy.com

www.document-strategy.com

About the Author

Kevin Craine, is the author of *Designing a Document Strategy* and the editor of *Document Processing Technology* magazine. His work has appeared in numerous document industry publications, technology journals and Web portals. With over 20 years experience in the field of information processing, Kevin is currently the manager of document services for Regence BlueCross BlueShield, the largest health insurance provider in the Pacific Northwest (USA). In addition, he is an adjunct instructor at Marylhurst University and a respected keynote speaker. Craine received his MBA in the management of science and technology, and his BA in organizational communications. For more information visit **www.document-strategy.com**.

Visit www.document-strategy.com

This web site is the place to visit for onging support and discussion regarding the design of a document strategy. Based on the book *Designing a Document Strategy*, by Kevin Craine, the web site provides a summary and outline of the book, chapter samples and a mailing list registration. As a member of the mailing list you will also have access to ongoing discusson, research and white papers that deal with the varied approaches and complicated issues surrounding the design of document strategy.

The need to implement a document strategy is a topic pursued with urgency in the field of information processing. But in spite of the industry buzz surrounding the subject, the inevitable lament is: "I know a document strategy is important, but how do I actually develop one?" The book, and the accompanying web site, provides a method and process to follow. As a result, whatever decisions and recommendations you ultimately make, they will be more likely to bring about real-world, bottom-line benefits.

Join the growing number of information professionals on the leading edge of document strategy design.

Other Titles from MC² Books

Designing a Document Strategy
by Kevin Craine

This book targets managers, technicians and consultants who see the benefit and cost savings inherent in implementing a document strategy. The 5-phase process is tailorable to any environment, and includes Cause-effect diagrams, flow charts, and ROI formulas to copy and use. Case examples apply the theories in the real world, leading to meaningful and informed action. With this book as a guide, readers will be more likely to bring about real-world, bottom-line benefits. There is no better educational resource on designing a document strategy than this book.

Only $29.95
plus shipping

Wrestling Legacy Data to the Web & Beyond: Practical Solutions for Managers & Technicians
by P.C. McGrew & W.D. McDaniel

Here's the book for everyone in the document chain, including managers, designers, strategists and print programmers. **Wrestling Legacy Data** gives you the background on line data, AFP and Metacode/DJDE print formats as well as PostScript, PCL and PDF. Learn the resource terms that will help you communicate effectively with your vendors, plus tips on resolving common problems, There is also an appendix of vendors from around the world who can help!

Only $29.95
plus shipping

The 48-Hour Rule and Other Strategies for Career Survival
by Lisa D. Magnuson

Want a bigger paycheck? More rewarding job? More recognition? You can have it if you know the rules! In this book Lisa D. Magnuson shares her expertise so that you can get your career on track. Using examples and sample plans, The 48-Hour Rule explains how to build better relationships with your co-workers and management, and how to sell yourself as opportunities come along.

Only $18.95
plus shipping

Critical Mass: A Primer for Living with the Future
by Pat McGrew & Bill McDaniel

Are you facing the technology squeeze? Adopt too early and the executives question your sanity. Adopt too late and you're called a dinosaur. This quick-to-read primer can help you make better decisions on the road to the future. There is no better resource for anyone who feels overwhelmed by the rapid pace of change and needs to find a baseline to understand how we evolved to where we are today.

Only $15.00
plus shipping

Please visit us at www.mc2books for more business titles and for titles in our popular culture imprints!